I0510811

# BITCOIN

*THE ULTIMATE GUIDE FROM BEGINNER TO EXPERT:*
*STEP-BY-STEP GUIDE FOR ENGINEERS, INVESTORS,*
*BUSINESS EXECUTIVES, AND NON-TECHNICAL USERS*

*BY RICHARD HAYEN*

Copyright © 2017 by Richard Hayen. All Rights Reserved.

This document is geared towards providing exact and reliable information in regards to the topic and issue covered. The publication is sold with the idea that the publisher is not required to render accounting, officially permitted, or otherwise, qualified services. If advice is necessary, legal or professional, a practiced individual in the profession should be ordered.

- From a Declaration of Principles which was accepted and approved equally by a Committee of the American Bar Association and a Committee of Publishers and Associations.

In no way is it legal to reproduce, duplicate, or transmit any part of this document in either electronic means or in printed format. Recording of this publication is strictly prohibited and any storage of this document is not allowed unless with written permission from the publisher. All rights reserved.

The information provided herein is stated to be truthful and consistent, in that any liability, in terms of inattention or otherwise, by any usage or abuse of any policies, processes, or directions contained within is the solitary and utter responsibility of the recipient reader. Under no circumstances will any legal responsibility or blame be held against the publisher for any reparation, damages, or monetary loss due to the information herein, either directly or indirectly.

Respective authors own all copyrights not held by the publisher.

The information herein is offered for informational purposes solely, and is universal as so. The presentation of the information is without contract or any type of guarantee assurance.

The trademarks that are used are without any consent, and the publication of the trademark is without permission or backing by the trademark owner. All trademarks and brands within this book are for clarifying purposes only and are the owned by the owners themselves, not affiliated with this document.

## Disclaimer

All rights reserved. No part of this publication may be reproduced, distributed, or transmitted in any form or by any means, including photocopying, recording, or other electronic or mechanical methods, without the prior written permission of the publisher, except in the case of brief quotations embodied in critical reviews and certain other noncommercial uses permitted by copyright law.

# TABLE OF CONTENTS

# INTRODUCTION

Congratulations on downloading your personal copy of Bitcoin: The Ultimate Guide From Beginner to Expert: Step-by-Step Guide for Engineers, Investors, Business Executives, and Non-Technical Users. Thank you for doing so.

The following chapters will discuss some of the many great things that you are able to do with the help of the bitcoin. The bitcoin is one of the best digital currencies that you are able to use in order to make purchases and sell things online. It isn't attached to any of the same things that traditional currencies that are out there, meaning that a government or a bank is not controlling it. This guidebook is going to talk a bit more about this as well as the different methods that you are able to make bitcoin to use.

Inside, we will talk a few the benefits of using the bitcoin system, as well as many of the ways that you are able to earn bitcoin for your own uses. We will talk about the process of mining the bitcoin, how to sell products to make bitcoin, investing options, and so much more. You can even take some of your traditional currency and exchange it for the bitcoin, just like you would with other exchanges and we will take a look at this as well.

Bitcoin is quickly becoming one of the best currencies to use all across the world and people love how it is secure to use, can help you to remain anonymous with some of the transactions that you do, and so much more. Make sure to read through this guidebook if you would like to start earning some of your own bitcoins with the help of mining, running your own business, and so much more.

There are plenty of books on this subject on the market, thanks again for choosing this one! Every effort was made to ensure it is full of as much useful information as possible. Please enjoy!

# CHAPTER 1: WHAT IS A BITCOIN?

There are several different types of currency that you are able to work with. Most countries are going to have their own forms of currency that are backed by the government, which allow people to make purchases and to pay for services. The bitcoin is similar to other currencies in that you are able to use it to get paid or to purchase services, but it is not controlled by any government or any other entity and there is no printed version. Rather, bitcoins are produced by people, and even by some businesses, and it is a form of cryptocurrency that has developed all on its own.

While you will find some differences in how bitcoins work compared to traditional forms of money, it is still able to work similar to traditional currency in that you are able to make purchases and use it to get paid. Of course, since there isn't a paper version, you will only be able to purchase the goods online rather than at a store, but it would work similar to how you would make other purchases online.

Bitcoin is a currency that is created as well as used digitally and it will be run by a big community that anyone throughout the world will be able to join. To get more of the bitcoin, you will be able to mine them or offer services while accepting payments with bitcoin. Inside of the bitcoin network, you can easily process transactions that would use the bitcoin as a form of payment, just like you would with credit cards or cash, which has helped to make bitcoin its own network of payment.

One of the reasons a lot of people like going with bitcoin instead of one of the other options is because it is decentralized. You aren't going to have to rely on a single institution like a government agency, to take care of the value of the money and you won't have anyone else messing around with the money, making it very valuable all throughout the world.

The bitcoin is not a currency that you are able to create and churn out more as you want. There are some rules in place for using the bitcoin and these state that you are only going to be able to find 21 million bitcoins that were created by the miners. You can divide up these bitcoins though so there may be more parts of the digital currency, but there is never going to be more than the 21 million bitcoin amount.

So the next question that you may have is what is the bitcoin based off? When we look at traditional forms of currency, such as the dollar bill in the United States, we would be able to take that currency to the bank and then we could, in theory, get that value back in gold. The bitcoin is not going to be based on silver and gold like most traditional currencies, but instead, since it is an online code, it is one that will be based on mathematics.

You will find that the software program for bitcoin is used all around the world and it is able to use some of the mathematical equations that Satoshi Nakamoto, the inventor of bitcoin, created. These mathematical formulas are easily available so that anyone is able to go into it and can work on the open sourced so that changes and adjustments can be done at any time.

## WHAT ARE SOME OF THE THINGS THAT MAKE BITCOIN SO GREAT?

There are many reasons that you will love being able to use bitcoin for making purchases or getting paid. Outside of being a great digital currency that you are able to use online, there are some other features that you will notice with bitcoin that help to set it apart from some of the other currencies that you would use including:

### *IT IS DECENTRALIZED*

The bitcoin is never controlled by a central authority. All of the machines that are able to mine the bitcoin and that are going to take care of the bitcoin transactions inside of the system will create their own network and will be able to work together. This means that there will not be a central authority that can come in and mess around with some of the policies or cause issues with the bitcoin. This authority is not able to make the bitcoins worthless and they can't take the money from you.

Even if this bitcoin network goes offline for some time, the money will keep on working.

## IT IS EASY TO SET UP

In some cases, you will find that it is difficult to get a bank account open or to get money from a bank in your area. But when you are working with bitcoin, you will find this is not such an issue. Users can set up their own bitcoin address in just a few seconds and you won't have to worry about the long list of questions or any fees that come with the traditional banks. None of this is needed to get started with bitcoin.

## YOU CAN BE ANONYMOUS

It is possible to be anonymous when you are working with bitcoin. You can pick out whether you would like to work with one address or more for your transactions, which can make it even harder for people to track what you are doing. Plus, your accounts are not going to be linked up to any of your personal information so you are able to work on this network and no one will be able to tell who you are.

## THERE IS PLENTY OF TRANSPARENCY

While you can stay anonymous on this system, you will find that bitcoin is going to store all of the details for all of their transactions on the network. This information will be stored in what is known as the blockchain and when you use a bitcoin address, anyone else will be able to see what is there. You are still protected by your address and you will be anonymous, but having bitcoin be transparent like this helps you to know that nothing shady is going on behind your back.

*TRANSACTIONS CAN BE FAST*

One of the reasons that people like to work with the bitcoin is because it is really fast for you to use it and see the transactions. Sometimes your traditional bank can take a few days in order to process the different things that you are doing, but bitcoin is almost instant. You can send out money from anywhere in the world and it only takes within a few minutes to get to the other person. This makes it faster to get the things that you are paying for and helps the seller to know that they are going to get paid in the process.

## HOW MUCH IS THIS BITCOIN WORTH?

For the most part, when you get paid with bitcoin, you will earn some part of the whole bitcoin, after it has been split up. You are able to split up the bitcoin quite a bit so that it is easier to make some of the purchases that you want on the network. Compared to other types of currencies, you will find that the bitcoin actually worth quite a bit of money. It will vary depending on what traditional currency we are talking about. For example, the bitcoin compared to the Euro was about $1134.84 and compared to the USD< it is worth $1,192.83.

Now, we talked about how it is only possible to create up to 21 million of the bitcoin, these are all worth a lot of money and it is likely that it will stick around for a long time. And as more people start to join this system, you will find that the bitcoin is going to go up even higher in value compared to the beginning.

The price of the bitcoin is going to vary based on which traditional currency you are basing it off of and how the bitcoin market is going to work. You will find that it is always varying, just like the traditional market, but it will not always change at the same time that the traditional market does. Make sure to check the exchange rate often to figure out how much your bitcoin is worth and how you will be able to use it on the network.

You will find that the bitcoin is a great currency to use online that will allow you to make some of the digital purchases that you want. It isn't going to be controlled by a government or another central agency, so it will not be messed with at all. You can even split it up into smaller bits to make some of the purchases that you like, all around the world, and you won't have to worry about the fees and other issues that come with traditional forms of currency.

# CHAPTER 2: HOW TO MINE YOUR BITCOIN

Now that we have a better idea of how bitcoin works, it is time to move on to how you can get started with bitcoin. There are a few different options, but we are going to talk about the process of mining. This is a good one to use if you want to get bitcoin and you have a little bit of experience when it comes to working in coding. When you work with some of the traditional sources of money, you will find that the government is in charge of printing more money when it is needed, but when it comes to bitcoin money, you will need to discover it when you want to create some more. There are a lot of computers all over the world and these can be used in order to mine the coins. Here we will take a look at some of the steps that you need in order to mine the bitcoin and when you are able to discover these coins, you will have some of your own.

## HOW DOES MINING TAKE PLACE?

In order for there to be more bitcoin, you will need to mine them. There is the maximum of 21 million of the bitcoin, but not all of them are in use right now. You may need to mine them in order to get more to go into the whole system. The process of mining is pretty simple, but you will need to work on it a little bit and it takes some time, which is why not everyone is going to choose this method.

Now, there are many people all throughout the world who will use this bitcoin network to send some of the bitcoins between each other, for making purchases and more. But without having some kind of record of these transactions, it is hard to keep track of which accounts have made the payments or not. Inside of the bitcoin network, there is a process for collecting the transactions that were able to happen during a set period, usually during one day, and then this information is going to be placed on a list.

For the system to keep track of the various transactions that will occur, which can often be a large list each day, a miner will be able to go through all of these and then confirm the transactions. They are able to take each individual transactions before writing them down onto a ledger.

## THE NEXT STEPS

So at this point, you may be uncertain about the point of the ledger. Why would you as a miner be so interested in learning this ledger and keeping track of it? The general ledger is going to be a long list of all the blocks that you use in this system. You are able to use this list in order to explore all of your transactions that are made between any of the addresses that you would like.

So on the blockchain, you are going to see all of the transactions that show up each day. As time goes on, this list will start to get fairly long because it will have lots of transactions that will show up over time. Anyone who is inside of the bitcoin network is going to be able to get a copy of this report so that they can decide to be a miner if they would like.

In order for this system to work, the general ledger needs to have some kind of process so that all of the users feel that their information is safe. This is where the miners are going to come into play. They are going to make sure to change the ledger in such a way that the information will stay safe and others won't be able to get the information.

When a new transaction block is created, it is going to be the job of a miner to put it through a process to keep things safe. They will help to take this information and then place it into a formula so that the information will be turned into something that is brand new. This is going to give you the results of something that seems random and is a lot shorter. You are basically going to include letters and numbers that are considered a has in this system. The hash will be stored inside of the block, somewhere near the end of the blockchain that you created.

You are going to notice that these hashes are able to have some cool properties. You can take some of this data inside the bitcoin block and it is pretty easy to make a hash from that information, but since this information will be random, it is almost impossible for others to come out and see what the data means. Each hash that is created will be unique and the nice thing is that they are able to take a big amount of data and give them their own unique hash so that it doesn't match up at all. For, example, if you are able to change up just a single character inside of the hash, you are going to be in a brand new transaction and it will look completely different.

Miners are not just taking the transactions in order to generate the new hashes. They are going to be able to use a little bit of information that is inside this data in order to help out. One important piece that you can use is the last block that is stored right at the end of the blockchain.

The neat thing is that each part or character of the hash is going to be used in order to produce the following one, you are going to get something completely unique each time. This helps to keep the security on these transactions because this method will help to create a wax seal inside of the digital world. The system will be able to look at the block, and the other blocks that are with it, and then if someone tries to tamper with the code, everyone inside of this network would find out quickly.

So if you are trying to be a miner and tried to fake one of these transactions, or you are trying to fake some for another reason inside of the system, you are going to have some issues. Even just changing one of the blocks that is in this chain is going to change up the whole block. If someone tried to see if the block was authentic with the hashing function, they would be able to see that something was changed and it is easy to see if the transaction is one that is false right away.

Since all of your hashes will be used with this same idea, with the character of one determining what the character of the next and all down the line, it is easier to see if someone is messing around with all of them, which helps them to stay safe.

It is the job of the miners to help keep track of all these different transactions inside of the system for bitcoin. They are going to be able to use an approach that is randomized and that can help to keep these transactions as secure as possible. In fact, if the job is done in the proper way, you will be able to see that all of the transactions will stay safe.

## HOW TO GET THE COINS

Now that we understand a bit about how hashes inside of the system and why all of this security is needed, it is time to work on what exactly a miner would do in order to compete and get some more of the coins. The miners are going to be the ones who are responsible for sealing off a block of the transaction with some randomized hashes so that they can compete with each other, using different types of software that has been designed for mining. And when they are able to create one of these blocks successfully, they are going to earn 25 bitcoins.

This is a great win for everyone. It is going to help those who are inside of the system stay safe ad secure so that people don't mess with the transactions or send out information that isn't true. It also helps the miner out because if they are successful, they are able to make some good money from these. Because of the high amount of money that you can make from these, you will find that many miners will work to create some more of these hashes and it can become very profitable.

The biggest issue is that the bitcoin network had to work to make things harder to create. In the beginning, people were able to just get a computer program and they were able to make money, but since this was so easy for a lot of people to do, so bitcoin had to make it a big harder to do.

There is now a process that is used that known as a proof of work that has helped it to become more difficult to create the hashes so that not all of the money in bitcoin could be mined in just a bit of time. The protocol with this network is going to help you to make sure that you meet everything when creating one of these hashes so that you can make some money. First, you should ensure that the hash looks a certain way in order to have a set amount of zeroes at the beginning. Since there is no way for you to know which way the hash will look until it is all done, you may have to make quite a few of them before you get it to work. And any time that you add in some more data to your system, it is going to change the hash up.

As the miner, you will make sure that you aren't going through and meddling around with the information that is with your transactions, but you will also need to make some changes in order to get your hash to become created and meet up with the rules. They are able to bring in another type of data, which is also going to be random so that you are able to create something that is known as a "nonce". This is going to be used as well as the data for the transaction so that you can make a brand new hash. So if you find that the data isn't fitting into the hash, the bitcoin will let you use the nonce so that you can change your hash around as well.

As you can imagine, the new rules make it so that you have to do quite a few tries to make sure that everything is going to work. But when you are willing to work with a computer program and keep on going with it, you can find that it is possible to make quite a bit of money with this mining option. The system is offering you $25000 USD for each of these hashes you are able to create, which means that if you are able to stick with it, it becomes possible to earn some good money. Make a few of these a year, and you have a good income.

Many people who are good with computer programming and like working with this kind of thing find that it is a great way for them to pick up a challenge and make some good money. If you like this idea, it is one of the best ways to go with to make some bitcoins without having to sell a product or do anything like that. Make sure that you have a good computer program that is able to help you to get started on this whole process of creating your own hashes.

# CHAPTER 3:

# WHAT CAN I USE THE BITCOIN FOR?

The nice thing about using the bitcoin is that you are able to use it for pretty much any purchase that you can with the USD or other traditional currencies. Some people are worried about the volatility of bitcoins because they find that there are big price differences that can make things difficult at times. But overall, there are many great benefits of using the bitcoin in order to make some of your payments online. Some of these benefits include:

- Fast transactions: for the most part, the transactions in bitcoin can be processed within 15 minutes. If you are working with a traditional bank you will find that these transfers can take a few hours, and sometimes it can take a few days to get the money from one of the accounts over to another. The bitcoin is able to get the transaction done in no time.

- Privacy: when you use the bitcoin network in order to make some transactions online, you will see that these are first registered with the blockchain. This is all public and you will be able to use some specialized websites in order to see if it is a valid transaction. Your name is not going to show up on any of these transactions, so you are able to make the purchases that you make so no one knows who is doing each one, keeping you safe and secure.

- Smaller commissions: you will not have to pay as much when it comes to using bitcoin for transactions. This is quite a bit lower compared to using the bank or PayPal in order to get things to work for the transactions. In addition, you only have to pay for this commission when you want to have a fast transaction, you could opt to have transactions take a few days, and then you won't have to pay for any of the commission at all, saving you a lot of time and money.

- Make many purchases: there are quite a few purchases that you are able to make when it comes to using the bitcoin. Some people go on this one in order to do some illegal transactions because of the anonymity that you are able to use on this system. But for the most part, people will choose to go with bitcoin in order to make things easier when you are traveling, to make purchases of items that you want, or even to sell some of the items that you want and be more attractive to your customers.

- Lending money: some people find that being able to lend money to others is a great thing to work with bitcoin on. You can lend money to others that you know or to someone else who is looking for a loan, and then charge some interest payments at the end. This makes it easier to see some results with your money working for you and is pretty simple when it comes to working in bitcoin.

- Do trading: some people decide to work with bitcoin because it is an easy way to do some trading and make some good money. You will be able to decide to do arbitrage and purchase an item that is really low on one site and then sell it for a higher price on another site. There are many options that come with trading, even day trading or holding onto the money for some time and waiting for the prices to go up, you just need to be a little bit creative with it and know how the bitcoin market works.

The bitcoin currency is one of the best digital currencies out there and many individuals and companies all throughout the world have come to using the bitcoin system to help you to make the purchases that you would like. Whether you want to use this in order to make some purchases or to make some money, you will find that bitcoin is one of the best options that you can go with no matter what.

# CHAPTER 4: HOW TO REMAIN ANONYMOUS WHILE USING BITCOIN

When it comes to using bitcoins, there are a lot of people who like to use it because it allows them to remain anonymous when they are completing their transactions. With credit cards and debit cards, there is always the worry that someone will be able to catch on to your information and know who you are, but thanks to the work that the miners do and your account not asking for personal information, the bitcoin trading system can be really great to keep anonymous. Even when you send the money to make purchases, it is possible to do this without the seller knowing who you are.

Being anonymous online in other method is pretty much impossible. But bitcoin has made it a bit easier because with the hashes that come with the transactions and the fact that you can have more than one account if you would like, you can make sure that your real life personality is not going to match up with your personal information, helping to keep your transactions, your personality, and so much more to help you to stay safe.

In order to make sure that your bitcoin account is safe and secure, there are a few more steps that you are able to take in order to keep this security when you make purchases. Some of the best steps for this include:

## STEP 1:

The first thing that you will need to do is get the Tails system and download it on your computer. You can look for it already on the Linux operating system, or you can use a DVD and a USB stick to put these on your computer as well. The best part is that Tails doesn't have to be downloaded on your computer to make it work, which is an extra security feature that is found with this system. You can just keep it on your USB stick and use it as needed.

Once the Tails system is all set up, you can route all of the traffic from the bitcoin network over through it. There are several ways that you can get ahold of the Tails software depending on how you would like to use it and what is easier for you. Sometimes you are even able to get it from a friend who will share or you can go to the Tails website. It is easy to work with Tails, and if you need to download it from the website, you will need to just follow the instructions and you are ready to go.

## STEP 2:

Once the Tails software is on the system, it is time to turn it on. If you got this from the Tails website, you are able to click right on the link, or you can insert the DVD or the USB that you want to use. If you find that the Tails program is already causing a bit of difficulty, you may need to work on the BIOS startup and you can use your persona to help with this. When creating this persona, remember that you don't want to have any personal information inside of it, or it kind of defeats the purpose of being unknown. In addition, you should be careful about keeping the documents, chats, and other things on topic if you want to see the results without someone finding out who you are. Also, when using this, make sure that you are closing up all of the social media accounts as well.

## STEP 3:

For this step, we are going to learn how to enable the persistence program. This is a good thing to do because it will help you to have all of the information for the program ready if you want to save any of your information on your Tails system. You should notice that there are an Applications heading in the program; click on here so that you are able to select on the Tails program before choosing which options you can configure.

If you want this option to work, you need to be on the USB drive in order to create a brand new program for the Tails Installer. If you worked with this stick manually, you will need to copy the Tails using a brand new USB drive to avoid issues or taking up too much space inside of the program. Then the Tails Installer is going to be pretty easy to work on because you are able to click on Applications, then Tails, and then Tails Installer. From here, you can pick out the passphrase that is easy for you to remember but is secure so that no one else is able to get onto the system.

During this process of installation, the Tails program is going to ask what information should be stored within the system. If you would like your Tails connection to stay secure, it is important that you keep the information that is stored on Tails pretty limited. The more information you place on there, the harder it is to get the Tails system set up and running and it is harder to keep your security in place.

Once you have picked out the right items that should be saved inside of the Tails system, you can restart the whole program, ensuring that persistence has been enabled. Then when the Tails system comes back up, make sure to enter the passphrase to get it all back on. Anything that you do from now on inside of the persistence folder can be saved and secure if you want to shut this computer down later on.

## STEP 4:

The next thing that we will need to work on is the PGP key. You will be able to create this new PGP key inside of the Tails program. You should be able to go into the Applications tab ad then over to Utilities before clicking on the Passwords and Keys part. Then you need to look for the plus (+) sin to help know that you are in the right place, and it is right under the GnuPG key?

Once you click on this button, it is time to enter your name and your email address when it is asked. Of course, make sure you are using the pseudonym that you already made up so that you are able to send off some emails that stay encrypted and which won't be easy for others to figure out who you are. The password is also going to be required and you will need to add it in each time that you are working on this section.

## STEP 5:

From this step, we are going to work on setting up a program that is known as Electrum. You will need to be able to get onto the Bitcoin Wallet and then click on the Applications. From here, it is possible to click on the Bitcoin Wallet and the Internet. You should think of the Electrum program like a light wallet that will work in bitcoin and here we are going to copy the blockchain so that we can use it later.

So when it is time to make the wallet that you would like to use with bitcoin, you will need to make sure that you are inside of the BlockCypher, which is also a good place to be when you would like to watch over the balance and the transactions of your bitcoin network. There isn't any need for you to go with other wallets besides the standard one in most places because you will see there is some security with them, but we will need to work on getting a password set up for this to keep it safe as well.

## STEP 6:

Now once all of this is set up, there are going to be times that it would be nice to communicate using this program. The nice thing is that it is possible to communicate when you are using the XMPP and the OTR to help with this communication. Pidgin is considered one of the best programs to use for this and it will allow you to communicate with any of the other users. The biggest issue that comes up with using this program though is that you need to be online if you would like to read any of the messages that you get, but otherwise it is one of the easiest programs to work with.

The Pidgin system will just need a few steps in order to get it installed. To do this, go and find the Applications tab and then get on the Internet before you decide to click on Pidgin. After you are here, you can access the Pidgin site by clicking on the account that you want to use, and then check the box that allows your protocol to be MPP.

You are not limited when you are using this program, which is something that a lot of people like about it. You are able to pick out the right search engine even for your communications. You also need a password to use this program, and then make sure that you click on the box that says "create a new account on server". Then when all of this is done, you need to close this window and then reconnect again so that your new chat is enabled with Pidgin. Keep in mind that when this window opens up again, the system will ask for the username and password again to make sure to keep those on hand anytime that you open up a new window.

Now, many people on the bitcoin system are going to have more than one account hooked up with this because it allows them to keep the accounts a bit more secure, rather than running the same things through them all of the time. The bitcoin system does allow you to have more than one of these accounts at a time, but if you would like to make sure that each of them is secure, you will need to go back through and do these steps all over again rather than trying to do it all with one system.

When you repeat these steps, you should make sure that each download of the Tails system is on a brand new USB drive so that you can keep everything separate and labeling is going to be your best friend here. They will each contain different keys for the PGP, different information, different databases, and even different passwords so make sure to keep it all separate and you can ensure that your account remains anonymous.

# CHAPTER 5:

# USING AN EXCHANGE TO GET BITCOIN

So far we have talked a bit about how to make sure that your account is safe from others and how to mine for some of the bitcoin that you want to use. But of course, it is not just computer programmers who are good at the mining options that will be able to join with the bitcoin system; there are some other options that you can use in order to get some of your own bitcoins and to start doing some of the trading that is needed.

Once you have been able to get the bitcoin all set up, it is time to go out there and get some of your own bitcoin. These are important so that you can make some purchases or get started on investing and other options that are inside this system. Now, if you have something for sale, you could choose to accept bitcoin as a payment and then have this available to help you out for starting bitcoin, but if you would like to make a purchase online using bitcoin, you would need to have some to start out with.

The good news is that you are able to take some of your current traditional currency and switch it over to bitcoin currency. There are a couple of good exchange sites that you are able to go with, which makes it easier to get right into the network. Let's take a look at some of the steps that you can take to start working wit bitcoin and ensuring that you can get into the market as well.

## WHICH EXCHANGE SERVICE SHOULD I USE?

So the first step here is to find one of the exchanges that you would like to use because this is the quickest way to get bitcoin; you will simply use this exchange in order to take some of your traditional currency, such as the USD, and then exchange it into bitcoin for you to use as you want. The bitcoin exchange is just like any other one that you will work with, such as if you were changing your USD over to CAD, and it is possible to use them to convert your money into real-time bitcoin. You will be able to find hundreds of these exchanges, but some of the best options include:

- **Xapo**: this is a company that provides debit cards as well as some wallets for bitcoin. You can use this in order to make some deposits of your personal traditional currency and then have it exchanged into bitcoin inside of your account.
- **Circle**: this is a good service that will help you to exchange, store, send, and even receive your bitcoins. It is only going to be able to work inside of the United States and it is necessary to hook up your bank account information with this service.
- **CoinBase**: this one is good for both the USD and the Euros. The company is one of the easiest for you to use

because it has helped out with the process of purchasing and trading both online and on your mobile phones.

Some of the exchanges that you use are just there to exchange currency for bitcoin while others are there to help act as a new wallet service and others will help with all the transactions and the trading and sell things you would like to do. For the most part, when you are using the wallets and the exchanges, you are going to store in some amount of digital currency so that you are able to work on making purchases in real time.

One thing to keep in mind here is that while you are able to be anonymous inside of the bitcoin system, you are still going to be required to show proof of identity just to get started with one of the exchange services. often the country that you live in is going to require some information as well to ensure that you are not trying to hide money from them when it is time for tax season.

## HOW TO USE THE EXCHANGE ACCOUNT

Once you have done all the steps to get your account set up, it is time to move the right money into the account so that your traditional money will become a bitcoin. All that you need to do here is link up your bank account to your bitcoin account so that you are able to move the funds over when you need them. You should note that this transaction between the bank and the bitcoin account is going to happen as a wire transfer and there is sometimes a small fee associated with that.

If you are worried about having the bitcoin account be attached to the bank account, you should consider opening a new account for this. You can just put in the money that you want to transfer open and leave it alone all of the other times. It is unlikely that someone is going to be able to get into your account, but having this precaution can really help to keep you safe. There are a few exchanges that make things even easier and will allow you to make some of your deposits in person or to use an ATM rather than having to do it all online. Also, when linking up a bank account, you will probably have to do it from the same country that the exchange is. So if you are using an exchange service inside of the United States, you will have to make sure that the bank account you are linking up comes from the United States as well.

## FINDING A SELLER

Some people like to find a seller in their area in order to exchange some of these bitcoins with. They are able to use some of their traditional currency and then will be able to trade with someone else to get the bitcoin. If you want to go with this option, you should use a site like LocalBitcoins, because it is one of the best for helping you to find people in your area who want to sell their bitcoins. Once you find a seller you would like to work with, you can meet with your seller face to face and then go through the negotiations of picking out the price that the bitcoins are worth.

Sometimes it is scary to think about meeting up with someone you don't know in order to exchange the bitcoin. For these people, you will be able to use a site like Meetup.com This allows you to find people who are selling their bitcoins, but you don't have to meet up with them, which can be nice if they are in another part of the country or the world. This one also works well if you can get together a group of people who want to purchase the bitcoins and then the whole group will make a decision on where to get the bitcoins.

If you do decide to meet up with some people in order to purchase bitcoins, you should have a good idea about how much you are willing to pay for them. You can go online and check the current rates for the bitcoin, so you know the amount that you will pay. In addition, sometimes the seller is going to charge you some sort of premium for the coins since they had to meet with you in person. Also, check with the seller you want to use and see if they would like a specific method of payment from you before getting started. Most traders are going to negotiate on the price a bit with you and most meetings are going to be pretty quick so that nothing happens in the bitcoin market before they get the money.

## CHECK OUT THE ATMS

Another option to get some bitcoins includes ATMs. There are a few of these already up, with more to come, and they are specifically meant to help you get more bitcoin. You will find that it is relatively new, but you are able to go online ad find if there are any ATMs in your area for you to use. Sometimes they are found at your local bank as well, depending on where you live and which bank you go to.

Keep in mind that when you are using one of these bitcoin ATMs, you will most likely need to use cash in order to make it work. Since you are only going to be able to use bitcoins in these machines, you are not able to work with a debit card or a credit card for these transactions. So basically, you are able to look for one of these machines in your area, and then just take out the cash that you would like.

In some cases, you are able to use one of the ATMs in your area in order to insert cash and get them onto your bitcoin account. You will then just need to have the QR code for your wallet and scan that into the ATM, or you can get the right code for the wallet through your own smartphone. This is one of the easiest ways that you can take some of the cash that you have and get it converted to bitcoin inside of your wallet online.

When it comes to using the ATMs, they can be really efficient, but you need to remember that the prices for doing these exchanges will vary based on which one you use. You are going to have to deal with the standard price of exchange that is out, but using these ATMs will often add another 3 to 8 percent on top of it all. This will make it more expensive to use compared to some of the other methods, but it is pretty easy to use and if you would like to just get the exchanges done in a quick manner for a purchase or to get started on the bitcoin network, this is the option to go with.

As you can see, there are quite a few methods that you are able to use in order to start using some of the bitcoins on the network. Some people like to work on their very own store and sell some of their own products to see results and others like the idea of mining the coins. But if you see something on the network that you want to purchase, you are able to just exchange the money that you already have and use that as bitcoin as well. The fact that there is already so many options when it comes to getting the bitcoins that you need is one of the reasons that so many people like this option.

Learning how to exchange out your money so that it works with the bitcoin system is one of the best ways to ensure that you are getting started. Most people will bring their own money onto the bitcoin system and then will work there, so finding a good exchange or a local ATM can be one of the best options to help you get started. Explore your options, compare some of the fees, and see what a difference it can make.

# CHAPTER 6: BEING A MERCHANT AND MAKING MORE BITCOIN

Since using bitcoin is relatively new, there aren't a lot of merchants who are taking these yet, but that is starting to change in many places. Many times you can choose whether you would like to accept this currency in your own business. While there are some disadvantages that do come with the bitcoin service, there are a lot of merits and it is growing quickly. Some businesses who want to be in the lead and beat out the competition will find that offering to accept bitcoin as a payment source may be the ones who are able to get ahead.

Setting up the bitcoin to work with your business is pretty simple. You would just need to set up your own wallet inside of the system and then request that you get a QR code scanner. The customer would then be able to use their own smartphone app in order to scan the QR code, which will contain all of the information that is needed for the transaction, and then the bitcoin amount will be moved over to the retailer. Just tapping on the confirm button would complete this transaction. If the user ends up not having any bitcoin inside of their account, the network will be able to convert dollars into this account and then transfer those to the digital currency.

This makes it pretty safe for you to work with. You just need to set up the QR code and then the customer will be able to pay you in this manner. You can also convert the bitcoin back into dollars any time that you want and often the processing fee is low, much lower than what you would find with credit cards. There is no risk of fraud, you will know that the payment processed through instantly, and you won't have to worry about hackers being able to steal some of the information, which is what makes this such a great program to use even as a business.

## USING BITCOINS IN THE HOSPITALITY INDUSTRY

Many companies in the hospitality industry will use the bitcoin to help customers' purchase their dining payments and for room payments. Guests will be able to bring out their mobile wallets or use a PC to the website in order to pay for the reservation online. You would need to use a third party BTC merchant processor to help handle some of these transactions. These kinds of clients are going to be installed on a tablet that the front desk of these establishments and then the customers will be able to make their payments.

Many in the hospitality industry like to use these because the transactions are fast and the processors are going to be able to take the bitcoins that you are using and transfer them into currency while also making a daily direct deposit into the bank account for the company, so they will be able to get their money right away without the worries.

Any form of hospitality, from food service to hotels and so much more, will be able to benefit from taking bitcoin. This can make it easier compared to having to wait for the payment to process in a few days, when the person is probably long gone, and can really help if you cater to people who are from other countries who aren't sure how to use the local currency. This is one of the biggest industries to take off with the bitcoin option and many places are already accepting this as one of their payment methods.

## USING THE BITCOINS FOR INTERNATIONAL TRAVEL

The use of bitcoins has been seen all throughout the world for but business and financial industries. In a world where people want something that is fast and convenient to use, the bitcoin is really handy and won't cause some of the hassles that other forms of currency give to you. Since bitcoins are considered a virtual currency, they are starting to replace some of the other options, such as the traditional bank notes, that are being used for payments all over the place.

The bitcoin has become so popular, that there are many banks and businesses that have their own awareness campaigns to help their customers to know about the bitcoin and encouraging them to use this form as a mode of payment in order to avoid the stress and to save them some time. The main advantage of using the bitcoin in business is that it allows you to always keep track of the exchange rates and transactions in the past of bitcoin.

When you do decide to travel, you will find that exchanging the currency all of the time, when you go between different countries especially, can be a big pain. The more destinations that you go with, the worse this situation is going to be. But when you choose to use the bitcoin, you are able to just use one form and get it to work at many different places, rather than having to switch them out all of the time.

When you trade out your cash all of the time for new forms of money in different countries, you will find that there are fees and other costs that can come up along the way. When you are able to use bitcoin no matter where you go, you are able to cut out some of these fees along the way. And since bitcoin is already fraud proof thanks to all of the cryptography with it, so you will not have to worry about any hacking with the bitcoin or your personal information getting taken.

As a seller, no matter where you are in the world, you will find that bitcoin can make sure that you get paid. There are times with other options of payments, you will be able to prevent people making a payment with you, getting their product, and then reversing the transaction. When it comes to using bitcoin, you will find that you are not able to reverse the transactions that you are doing. This is great for ensuring that you as a seller will be able to get the payments that you deserve.

There are many different kinds of businesses who are going to be able to use bitcoin to help them to get the results that they would like. Any company is able to use the bitcoin service and this can help to give them some of the competitive edges that they are looking for in the long run. You just need to get the right codes in place and then your customers will be able to make payments with their smartphones. You will be able to keep them in the form of a bitcoin or get them transferred over. The payments ca be done in just in a few minutes so you don't have to wait. Not only is the bitcoin a great way for the customers to make payments, but can be great for the sellers to get their money in no time as well.

# Chapter 7: Other Ways to Make Money with Bitcoin

There are many methods that you can use in order to make some money using bitcoin. Whether you have some to get started with or you are looking to move your business onto using the bitcoin, you will want to find some more of the methods that you are able to use in order to make some extra money with the bitcoin. In order to be able to sell your own services and products online and accepting bitcoin as a payment, there are also some other methods that are used in order to make the purchases that you want on the network or to earn an income. You can do things such as trading the bitcoin or lending them out to some others to help them out. Now let's take some time to look at some of the different methods that you can use in order to make some more money with the help of bitcoin.

## Trading and Earning Bitcoin

One of the options that you can choose to earn some more bitcoin includes trading. With this, you are working for a form of gambling, so rushing into it and not thinking things through or really learning how to make it work can cost you a lot of money. When it comes to gambling, though, as long as the game is fair, you will have a set probability of winning or losing based on the game that you are playing. But when it comes to trading some of the assets, you will find that there are some more complex issues that come with it.

The best way to work with trading and then make some money with bitcoin in this manner is to use arbitrage. With this process, you are going to see that there is some kind of new opportunity in order to purchase a new asset at one location for a low price, knowing that as soon as you are done with that purchase, you can take it over to another market and make a big profit because it is selling for higher over there. You need to know, before making the purchase, that you will be able to make the profit, otherwise, you can easily waste your money with this one. If you end up making some purchases without having any ideas of whether you are able to make a profit from it, you will be gambling and it is unlikely that you can make a profit.

There are a lot of arbitrage situations that are open for you to use. Many times the trader is going to be on a few different sites that they want to use, and they will notice that on one site, there is a product that is offered for one price, but then on the second site, it is offered for quite a bit more. The trader would make the purchase on the first site and then turn around and make the sale on the second site in order to make a profit in the process.

But there is often a little bit more that goes with this as well. You need to be able to recognize what the value of the product is all about so that you can tell if you are getting a good deal or if you will be able to actually sell it for a profit on the other site. If you are good at working in business and figuring out how all of this comes together, this is a great option to go with, but it is not as simple as a quick purchase and a quick sale in order to make the money.

Some simple speculation is often used when it comes to trading that works along with bitcoin. With the speculation, you are going to make a purchase of bitcoins at one price, and then you will just hold onto them without using them until you notice that the price is starting to increase. You will then be able to sell the bitcoin when the price goes higher, therefore making a profit. You would want to do this whenever the bitcoins are at a low and then sell them once you see that the prices are going up.

For this one to work, you need to be good at guessing how the market for bitcoins is going to work; the trick here can be that this won't always work like the traditional currencies are so you can't always go by that either. When you know the market for bitcoin pretty well, you will have a better chance at guessing the accuracy of where the bitcoin will go, otherwise, you will just end up losing money in the process.

Any time that you want to get into the process of trading, you will need to get good at reading the market for bitcoin and recognizing some of the patterns that will occur. This is kind of specialized work and you will find that not everyone is going to do a good job with it. Trading is a great way to make some money with bitcoin, but you need to understand how the market will work and you need to make good decisions to see this happen.

## EARNING MONEY ON INTEREST WITH BITCOINS

If you already have some bitcoins on you, you may want to try putting some of these to work for you. You could decide to lend out these bitcoins, just like you would do when it comes to lending out your traditional money, and then earn some money from the interest that is charged in the process. You can lend these out to some other companies or to other individuals to help them get started, and then charge the interest that you would like in order to make some income in the process. There are a few different options that you can get when it comes to working with making interest with bitcoin including:

### DIRECT LENDING

The first one we are going to work with is direct lending. With this method, you will find someone you already know and lend them the money to help you to earn something back. Since you already are familiar with this person, you will be able to figure out if they are a good person to lend to and if you will be able to get this money back. Both parties will need to come together in order to come up with the terms of this agreement, such as how much the other person is going to pay in interest and how long they have to pay the whole loan back. In many cases, you probably don't have a lot of people you are close to that would like to borrow bitcoins, but it is certainly a place to look.

*PEER TO PEER LENDING*

Another option that you can go with is known as peer to peer lending. You will be able to find some websites that include a list of borrowers, all of whom are looking for a lender to give them some money. The borrowers are going to be able to list out their requests for funding, and they will usually include some information on how they will use the money. Then as the lender, you can determine if you will give them a portion of that money or all of it, based on how much you want to lend and the amount that you want to give them.

Depending on how much you give the borrower, you will earn a percentage on the interest payments each month. You will be able to look over the reason that someone is requesting the loan (such as what they are going to use the money for), the terms for interest payments, and even some of the other lenders to help you to make some better choices. Be careful with lending this way; it can make you some good money, but only if you pick out a few good borrowers to work with.

*WORK WITH A BITCOIN BANK*

For this particular option, you will be able to take some of the bitcoins that you are looking to deposit and you will place them into a bank. When you leave them there, the bank will pay you a little bit of an interest rate on any amount that you leave in there. This method will make it more likely that you will make some sort of return on investment, and the percentage amount is going to be determined right from the beginning, but remember that your return on investment is going to be a bit lower compared to some of the other options.

The reason that a lot of people like this option is because they are able to leave their money with a bank, which is often more trustworthy compared to some of the other options. The bank will pick who to lend to and can often do a better job at this than you can when picking out good people as borrowers. You may not make as much money as some others will with this option, but it is a good secure investment that can help you to build up a bit of your currency ahead od time.

## SELL YOUR PRODUCTS OR SERVICES

Any time that you are able to provide a product or a service to others, you are able to use bitcoin in order to accept some payments on the system. It is easy to make bitcoin a simple addition to your accepted payments and you will be able to get ahead of some of your competitors when you are able to do this. You should take the time to see what the current exchange rates are for bitcoin and whatever traditional currency you usually use because this will help you to come up with the price point that is good for your needs, and it ensures that you are not having to go crazy with the payments because you don't know what you are doing.

When you choose to have people pay you with bitcoin rather than with just traditional currency, you are basically helping your money to grow because it is going to grow with the rising value of the bitcoin. This will help you to make sure that you are able to earn more money because it is likely that the value of the bitcoin is going to rise in the coming years, so this will really help you out.

*DAY TRADING*

This is another option that you are able to go with and it is going to be similar to selling the bitcoin right after you get it. This is the act of getting a bitcoin and then selling it within a day of owning it. In order to technically be doing day trading, you will have to make the purchase as well as the sales all on the same day, and you will be able to take advantage o the lowest as well as the highest average prices during the day. You will find that with day trading you are not going to get the best return on investment each day for the long term, but you can earn a lot of smaller returns in the day and this can add up over time.

In order to do the day trading, you will need to be able to find the lowest price on the day because this is going to be the time when you will need to purchase the bitcoin. So let's say that the lowest price of our day is $913. You would want to make a purchase of the bitcoin while it is there, and make sure that you are not spending more than the $913 on it. You would then be able to keep track of the prices for the rest of the day and find when the highest one occurs. For our example, let's say that is $933. You would then be able to sell the bitcoin during that point and make $20.

The more of the bitcoin that you are able to sell and buy, the more you are able to make a good profit from this option. If you are working with five different bitcoins in the example above, you would basically make $100. As you can see, the profits on one are not very big, but they do add up pretty quickly when you are able to purchase more and when you can keep doing this over time. The returns are low, but they will help you out.

It is even possible to watch the prices, and if you see that one drops through the day, it is possible to repurchase that same bitcoin and end up making some more money from it. This is a good think because if you find that the prices are dropping by quite a bit during the day, you can make sure that you still see some profits from these drops.

Day trading can end up making you a lot of money in the long run, but you really need to know what you are doing. It is not a good idea to just jump in because the market is going to work differently than what you are used to. When it comes to working with bitcoin, it is not going to work like some of the other options do. But if you are able to spend some time learning about the market and learning about how to do some of the trades with the bitcoin network, this can easily become a great way for you to make some great money as well.

As you can see, there are quite a few options that you can work with in order to make some money with the help of the bitcoin system. It is often your own personal choices and what you are most interested in that will help you to determine which of these will be your way to get into this digital currency and start making some of your own money.

# CONCLUSION

Thank for making it through to the end of Bitcoin: The Ultimate Guide From Beginner to Expert: Step-by-Step Guide for Engineers, Investors, Business Executives, and Non-Technical Users. Let's hope it was informative and able to provide you with all of the tools you need to achieve your goals.

The next step is to get started on using the bitcoin system for your own needs. Whether you are looking to start your own business (or at least grow it with some more customers) or you would like to be able to make some of your own purchases, you are going to find that bitcoin can be there to help you out. This guidebook is going to help you to learn more about the bitcoin system and all of the neat things that you are able to do with it.

Make sure to take a look through this guidebook and learn all that you can about how to make purchases and sell things with the help of the digital currency known as bitcoin.

Finally, if you found this book useful in any way, a review on Amazon is always appreciated!

www.ingramcontent.com/pod-product-compliance
Lightning Source LLC
Chambersburg PA
CBHW051249170526
45165CB00004B/1638